One third of the average dump is made up of packaging material.

If every Sunday n[...] United States was recy[...], 250 million trees a year would be saved.

Disposable diapers take 500 years to decompose.

Between Thanksgiving and New Year's, Americans throw away up to 4 million tons of wrapping paper and shopping bags.

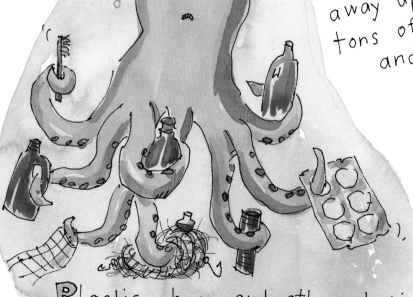

Plastic bags and other plastic garbage thrown in oceans kill as many as 1 million sea creatures every year.

STAGE 2

What Happens to Our TRASH?

by D. J. Ward • illustrated by Paul Meisel

Collins

An Imprint of HarperCollinsPublishers

Special thanks to Mark A. Cane, G. Unger Vetlesen Professor of Earth and Climate Sciences, Lamont-Doherty Earth Observatory of Columbia University, for his valuable assistance.

The Let's-Read-and-Find-Out Science book series was originated by Dr. Franklyn M. Branley, Astronomer Emeritus and former Chairman of the American Museum–Hayden Planetarium, and was formerly co-edited by him and Dr. Roma Gans, Professor Emeritus of Childhood Education, Teachers College, Columbia University. Text and illustrations for each of the books in the series are checked for accuracy by an expert in the relevant field. For more information about Let's-Read-and-Find-Out Science books, write to HarperCollins Children's Books, 10 East 53rd Street, New York, NY 10022, or visit our website at www.letsreadandfindout.com.

Let's-Read-and-Find-Out Science® is a trademark of HarperCollins Publishers.
Collins is an imprint of HarperCollins Publishers.

What Happens to Our Trash?
Text copyright © 2012 by D. J. Ward
Illustrations copyright © 2012 by Paul Meisel
All rights reserved. Manufactured in China.
No part of this book may be used or reproduced in any manner whatsoever without written permission except in the case of brief quotations embodied in critical articles and reviews.
For information address HarperCollins Children's Books, a division of HarperCollins Publishers, 10 East 53rd Street, New York, NY 10022.
www.harpercollinschildrens.com

Library of Congress Cataloging-in-Publication Data is available.
ISBN 978-0-06-168756-3 (trade bdg.) — ISBN 978-0-06-168755-6 (pbk.)

12 13 14 15 SCP 10 9 8 7 6 5 4 3 2
❖
First Edition

WELCOME TO COMMUNITY PARK

FORMER TOWN LANDFILL

To Keaton and Audrey —D.J.W.

To Phoebe Yeh —P.M.

ACME
WASTE

HOUSEHOLD
TRASH

Have you ever looked inside a garbage can? Hold your nose! It might be stinky. There are all kinds of things in there! It is all stuff people have thrown away. It's trash.

A lot of what people throw away is paper and cardboard. Some of it is plastic—bottles, packages, and even toys. People throw away TVs and bicycles. Metal cans and glass bottles. Furniture and clothing. Food scraps, grass clippings, and oily rags. Some of it is so gooey and grimy, it's hard to tell what it is. What do you throw away?

In the United States, we make a lot of trash. We make more than any other country. We make almost five pounds per person every day.

Most of our trash goes to a landfill. Landfills are areas set aside for storing trash. Big cities usually have at least one.

Putting waste into a landfill is different than just placing it in piles and leaving it. That would smell bad and be unsafe. It would attract animals and flies. It could make people sick. Landfills are made to keep people safe from the trash.

Landfills have clay and plastic layers. This helps keep harmful liquids from leaking away. The trash gets covered with dirt each day.

When trash sits in a landfill, it makes gases. Pipes at the landfill capture the gases, keeping them from polluting the air.

One kind of gas the pipes capture is called methane. People burn the methane to make electricity for their houses, schools, and office buildings.

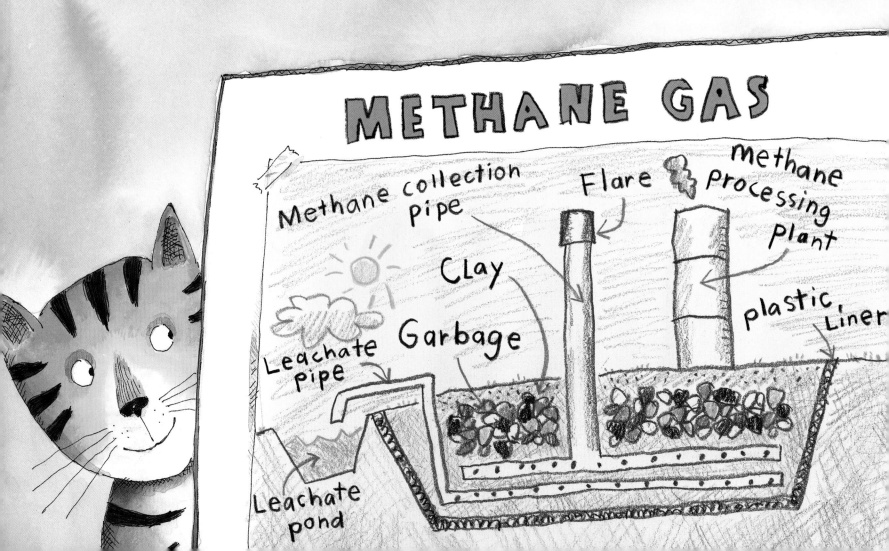

METHANE GAS

Methane collection pipe

Flare

methane processing plant

Clay

Garbage

Leachate pipe

plastic liner

Leachate pond

Some trash is too dangerous to go straight into a landfill. Batteries, some cleaners, and compact fluorescent lightbulbs contain chemicals that could hurt people. They are called household hazardous waste.

You should not put this kind of trash into your garbage can at home. Many cities have drop-off sites for household hazardous waste. This is where workers place the waste in containers that get sealed up tight. Now the household hazardous waste can go safely into the landfill.

One day, the landfill will run out of space for more trash. When a landfill becomes full, workers carefully cover it. They plant grass on it. The landfill becomes a park. It might even become a golf course. The trash is still down below. It takes some kinds of trash a long, long time to break down. Hundreds or thousands of years, even!

TRASH

Sometimes it is hard for cities to find a place to put trash. Landfills take up a lot of space. And they can't be near people's homes or where they might harm wildlife. Some cities send their trash to faraway landfills. But that costs a lot of money.

To save space in landfills, some cities burn their trash. Heat energy from the fire can be used to turn turbines. As the turbines turn, they make electricity. That puts the trash to good use. But burning trash causes problems, too. It can pollute the air. And it's expensive.

Whether we bury it or burn it, keeping people safe from trash costs a lot of money. The more trash we make, the more trouble it can be.

So what can we do to stop throwing away so much stuff? We can reduce, reuse, and recycle!

To reduce means to make smaller. What if each person made only four pounds of trash every day? Or maybe only three? Landfills wouldn't fill up so quickly. There would be less pollution in the air from burning trash.

Making less trash is not hard to do. But to do it we have to change some habits. We can bring our own bags to the store and use them instead of throwaway bags.

We can buy a big bag of snacks instead of lots of little bags. The little ones make more trash. Snacks for lunch can go into a reusable container from home.

We can use rechargeable batteries instead of the disposable kind.

To reuse means to use something more than once. What kinds of things can we reuse?

A lot of the trash in landfills is old containers. But many of those containers could have been used again. Clean boxes are useful for organizing toys and making crafts. You can reuse plastic food containers for storing leftovers. Just make sure they're clean first! When we use plastic forks, spoons, knives, cups, and plates, we can wash them and use them again.

Used office paper often has printing only on one side. We can print on it again or draw on the blank side.

Some things we throw away might be useful to somebody else. We can take toys and clothes we don't use anymore to the thrift store.

Some kinds of trash can be turned into something else that is useful. Yard waste and food waste are like that.

Yard waste is from plants. Grass clippings, branches, and leaves are all examples of yard waste.

Food waste is from meals. When you make a meal, some parts of the food don't get used. Things such as eggshells, melon rinds, and apple cores all go into the trash. After the meal, food is sometimes left on people's plates. That's all trash.

When yard waste and food waste decay, they become plant food. That's called fertilizer. Making fertilizer from yard and food waste is called composting.

Some cities collect yard and food waste for composting. Does your town have compost piles? You can ask your parents or teachers, or check online to find out.

Even if your town does not have compost piles, your yard and food waste doesn't have to go to the landfill. You can set up a compost pile at home.

Using compost on your plants and lawn can help reduce the need for chemical fertilizers and decrease pests and disease.

What if we could take the plastic from a bottle and make carpet for the floor? Or what if we could turn old newspaper into a new cereal box? We can! It's called recycling. To recycle means to use the materials from one thing to make something else. Some countries recycle almost half their trash. Why can't we?

towels

Some things made from recycled materials.

furniture

books and magazines

NATURE

Fruity cereal

packaging

jewelry, bags, clothing

building materials

shoes

carpets

Lots of items can be recycled, such as plastic containers, glass bottles, and metal cans. We can recycle many kinds of paper: cardboard boxes, printer paper, and newspapers. Magazines, catalogs, and phone books. Even ads that come in the mail.

29

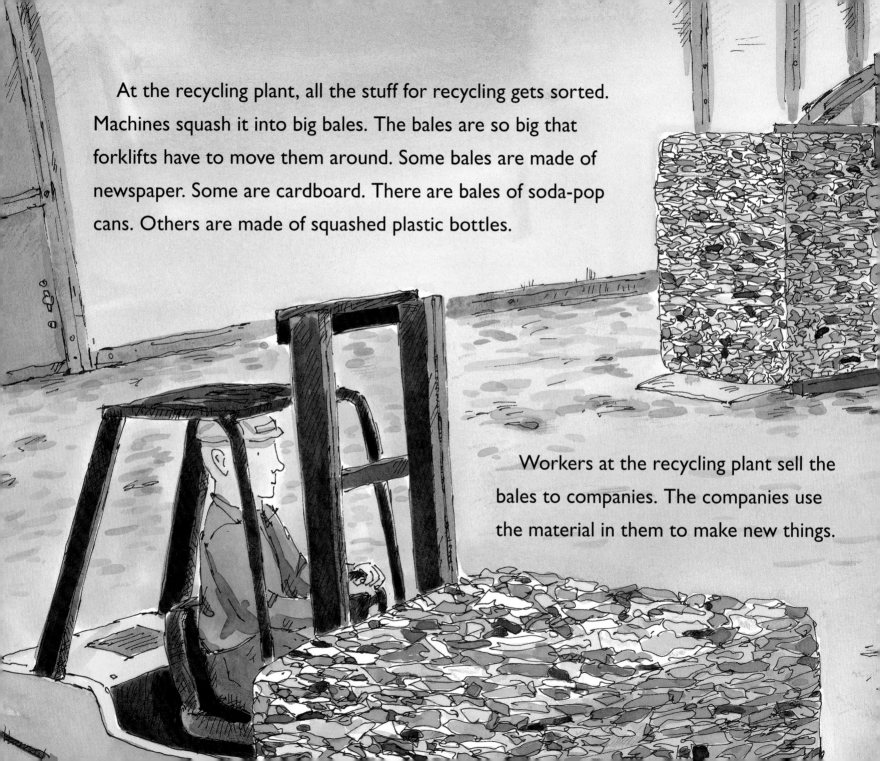

At the recycling plant, all the stuff for recycling gets sorted. Machines squash it into big bales. The bales are so big that forklifts have to move them around. Some bales are made of newspaper. Some are cardboard. There are bales of soda-pop cans. Others are made of squashed plastic bottles.

Workers at the recycling plant sell the bales to companies. The companies use the material in them to make new things.

Machine
that makes
bales

Bales of
recycled
material
are shipped
all around
the world
to make
new things.

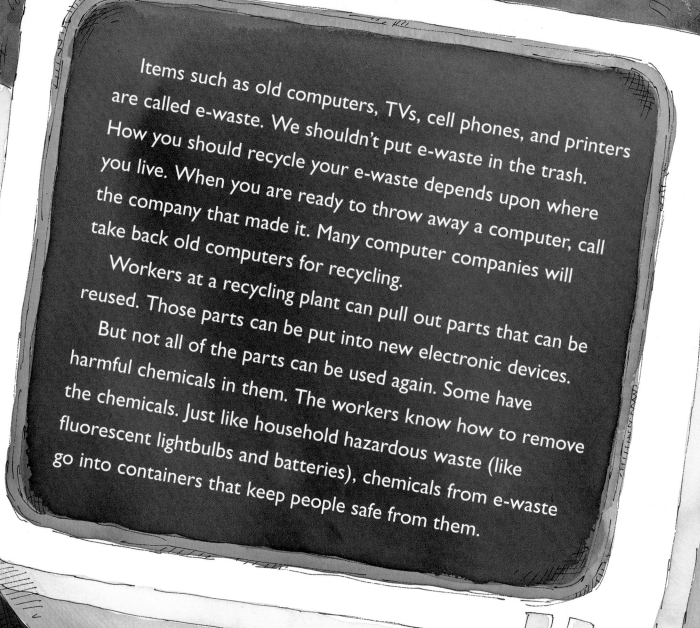

Items such as old computers, TVs, cell phones, and printers are called e-waste. We shouldn't put e-waste in the trash. How you should recycle your e-waste depends upon where you live. When you are ready to throw away a computer, call the company that made it. Many computer companies will take back old computers for recycling.

Workers at a recycling plant can pull out parts that can be reused. Those parts can be put into new electronic devices. But not all of the parts can be used again. Some have harmful chemicals in them. The workers know how to remove the chemicals. Just like household hazardous waste (like fluorescent lightbulbs and batteries), chemicals from e-waste go into containers that keep people safe from them.

So where will your trash go? Will it go to the recycling plant? Will it go to the compost pile? Will it get buried underground?

It's almost impossible to make no trash at all. But if we reduce, reuse, and recycle, we will make a lot less than we do now.

And a lot less trash will go to the landfill! That's one great way to help make where we live a cleaner, greener place.

Find Out More About Trash

Create Your Own Compost Pile

You can create a compost pile in your backyard or indoors. If you don't have space for an outdoor compost pile, you can compost indoors, too. You'll need a special type of bin, which you can buy or make yourself. If you take care of it, it won't attract bugs. It won't smell bad either. You can put lots of things in it—grass, leaves, eggshells, apple cores, sawdust—even lint from the dryer. The compost pile will turn the trash into plant food. You can use the compost you make for planting things. All composting requires three basic ingredients:

- Browns (dead leaves, branches, twigs) provide carbon for your compost.
- Greens (grass clippings, vegetable waste, fruit scraps, coffee grounds) provide nitrogen.
- Water provides moisture to help break things down.

Here's one way to make a backyard composting pile:

- Pick a dry, shady spot near a water source.
- First, chop or shred your brown and green materials.
- Next, use your brown materials to cover the bottom of your composting area with a 6-inch layer.
- Then, add a 3-inch layer of green materials and some soil.
- Use a pitchfork to lightly mix the two layers.
- On top, add a 3-inch layer of brown materials.
- Add water until the pile is moist.
- Turn your compost pile every week or two. This will distribute air and moisture.
- Move dry materials from the edges into the middle of the pile.
- Your compost will be ready in one to four months.

For more information on composting, visit www.epa.gov/epawaste/conserve/rrr/composting/by_compost.htm.

Trash Facts

In the United States, most of our trash is made up of paper and paperboard. Want to learn more about what we throw away?
Visit www.epa.gov/osw/conserve/materials/organics/food/fd-basic.htm.

People in Germany and Sweden make about half as much trash in a day than people in the United States. How does the United States compare to other countries when it comes to making trash and recycling? Find out by visiting www.epa.gov/region4/recycle/faqs.htm.

You can find out more about recycling from these websites:

- EPA Planet Protectors Club for Kids:
  www.epa.gov/epawaste/education/kids/planetprotectors
- Kids Recycle!: www.kidsrecycle.org
- Kids' Recycling Zone: www.kidsrecyclingzone.com

Some states have their own recycling websites for kids. You can find out if yours has a website by typing the words "recycling" and "kids," along with the name of your state, into an internet search window. Here are just a few:

- Wisconsin Department of Natural Resources: www.dnr.state.wi.us/org/caer/ce/eek/earth/recycle/index.htm
- Texas Commission on Environmental Quality: www.takecareoftexas.org/for-kids
- California's Department of Resources Recycling and Recovery (CalRecycle): www.calrecycle.ca.gov/kids
- Massachusetts Department of Environmental Protection: www.mass.gov/dep/recycle/reduce/kidsteac.htm

An estimated 80 million Hershey's Kisses are wrapped each day, using enough aluminum foil to cover over 50 acres — that's almost 40 football fields. All that foil is recyclable, but not many people realize it.

Some kinds of plastic can be recycled into fleece, fiber, tote bags, furniture, carpet, paneling, straps, and more.

Food waste from cafeterias, kitchens, restaurants, and fast food chains makes up about 1/8 of all trash.

If a single quart of motor oil is not disposed of properly, it can contaminate 2 million gallons of freshwater.

A bottle takes 4,000 years to decompose.